# maybe we were meant to be maybe

# maybe we were meant to be maybe

Damaris Bromeis

Bibliografische Information der Deutschen Nationalbibliothek:
Die Deutsche Nationalbibliothek verzeichnet diese Publikation in der Deutschen Nationalbibliografie; detaillierte bibliografische Daten sind im Internet über http://dnb.dnb.de abrufbar.



Herstellung und Verlag: BoD – Books on Demand, Norderstedt

ISBN: 978-3-7519-8251-1

# table of time

# twenty sixteen

## June $28^{th}$

am I lying to myself? when I say I just want everyone to be happy? don't I just want me to be happy? I had everything I wanted, I played with them. now they're gone, and now I see how much I loved them. they promised. I knew they were lying. I believed. and I knew. but I believed. because I wanted to. I thought I couldn't lose them. now they're gone. and I miss them. it's never going to be like it was before. I want to cry. I like them. I really do, I like them way more than they ever liked me. and I knew. I wanted to believe, when they said they liked me. but I knew. and I still believed. but no, I'm not lying to myself. I want every single one of them to be happy. and even if it's not with me, I want them to be happy. with all of my heart. because I will always be here and I will always love them.

<u>10:20PM</u>

you are my happiness. now I feel you going, going away from me, slowly drifting away from me. you were here, and you cared, and I never had someone like you. and maybe I'm overreacting, again. but I just care about you. I want you, like you used to want me when I took you for granted. and now I feel you going, going away from me, slowly drifting away from me. but I don't feel like I'm overreacting, again. because I just care about you. I knew how much you wanted me, as much as I want you now, now you take me for granted. I was your happiness. and I know you loved me. and maybe, just maybe, I love you now.

10:29PM

when did you become a crush? hoping it to be you when my phone rings or when I get a message. hoping to accidentally touch you in the hallways. wanting to spend the rest of my life with you. missing you, even though you're not even gone. remembering every single conversation we had, because they are so rare. when did I start loving you?

July 30th

10:17AM

it doesn't matter who you were before you changed

August 13th

<u>1:03AM</u>
and I've never felt this alone before

<u>7:14PM</u>
it just didn't work out. but you know that it could have.

November 14th

5:46PM
you'll get him.
you're the kind of girl who likes glitter and the color purple.
you’re the princess kind of girl.
you're the kind of girl who gets the prince.
you'll get him.

November 21$^{st}$

1:28AM

your words jump forwards while your actions go backwards

5:44PM

I told you I wanted a break from our friendship because I thought it might not be good for us anymore. so why does this feel like a break up?

twenty
seventeen

March 15th

11:15AM

I always thought we were meant to be. like, one day we will be together anyway, we just need the time to realize. but now I see each other drifting apart, wondering if it's a test or a sign to let go. is he really the one for me or is he just a good part of my life? I always saw something special in our relation to each other, something that wasn't normal and everyone else saw it too. but now I wonder if we are just stones in each other's ways. I don't want to let go, I love him. but this time I really don't know what the right thing is. fight or let go? what is the right thing to do? if I only followed my heart I'd forgive him everything. am I only imagining us drifting apart? I don't know what to think but I know what I feel. I feel lots of love, disappointment and fear that this time, it's the end.

April 29th

1:48PM

you used to say you aren't responsible for my problems but now that you're gone, I must say I don't have problems anymore.

1:59PM

it's over. now that it's definitely over I don't know what to feel. I am sad, because we lost what we once had and it was valuable. but I also feel free- like I can finally let go and like I can restart now and become a better person full of love. cut and dye my hair, redo my room and concentrate on friends who care. be happy again. Start seeing the colors of the world again. because he doesn't deserve a girl who loved him so much her world turned gray. what he really deserves is to see how the girl he lost becomes pretty and happy, and that maybe one day he realizes what he lost. and maybe one day he regrets letting her go. he let a girl go who loved him. he let me go.

May 22nd

<u>12:53AM</u>

you can break my heart but don't steal my fucking sleep.

June 4th

<u>4:23PM</u>
don't worry. we'll find each other again.

June 7th

9:23PM
and I have never been happier.

June 16th

10:51PM

I miss you

July 28$^{th}$

2:17PM

and you know that I don't want you to go

July 31st

<u>4:08PM</u>

no matter how it's going to happen- one day, I'll be happy. I will fall in love. maybe I'll have a family and maybe I'll have figured it out. one day, there will be a moment when I am truly happy. and this moment is worth living for.

August 4th

<u>6:30AM</u>
the bravest thing I ever did was run
cause you would have never thought I would

August 6th

<u>10:43PM</u>
did you already know this was going to happen when you didn't want to promise me forever?

<u>10:44PM</u>

you never wanted to promise me we were forever and now I know why

August 11th

<u>12:11AM</u>
and I don't know why all my poems are still about you
but I know my life and my thoughts aren't

## August 12th

<u>8:31PM</u>

I burned all the bridges so if you want me, I guess you'll have to swim.

August 17th

<u>11:19PM</u>

you were that one piece in the puzzle I thought was right until I looked closer and noticed you were wrong all the time.

September 15th

6:25PM
no one gives a fuck anyway

November 6th

1:17PM
the only one stopping me was myself so I got out of my fucking way

November 11$^{th}$

<u>12:18AM</u>
what is this supposed to be

November 26th

2:53AM

he told me I'm a beautiful woman
and that I can be my own idol
and that I'm wonderful
and he likes me just because I'm me
and that it doesn't matter if I'm struggling sometimes
and that he's going to help me.

December 10th

9:54PM
and if the fight never ends, I guess I'll always be winning then.

December 23rd

<u>2:46AM</u>

a new year is just around the corner. an official new beginning for everyone, for you too. you don't have to be like that. you aren't your flaws, your depression or your eating disorder. you know who you are. you just don't know how to wake up the real you, because you're too intoxicated by all the hatred. but that doesn't mean you'll never live up to your fullest. energy. love. growth. beauty. you are all of that, you just can't show it because there's too much dust all over you. you are amazing, every single cell of your body loves you, other people love you, and whatever possible god there might be loves you too. this isn't recovering or running away. this is discovering how strong you can be, growing to be even greater than you already are. this is exploding and letting out all of the good things you're holding inside of you. you are good enough, and there is a reason you were born. there is so much time for you left to live. so live, because you were given the opportunity to. you can do everything, you just have to believe. suicide is not how the strongest people go. the strongest people leave with a smile, knowing that nobody else would be able to survive what you survived. you were always enough. whoever says differently is a liar. you are supposed to live, love and give.

nothing is ever an act of weakness. there is always strength in weakness. if you ever think you‘re weak- you‘re not. the moment you feel the weakest, you already survived so many moments of strength and exhaustion. at that point you‘re actually the strongest. because it may have weakened you. but it has still not beaten you. and you know it never will.

this new year will be no different from the old one. but you will be a lot different.

December 26th

12:35AM
look- if you‘re going to do this I‘m in. but I‘m not going to play games.

twenty
eighteen

March 18th

10:08AM

I was afraid to lose you so I faced my fears and left

March 27th

<u>11:01PM</u>

want me when I no longer want to be wanted
want me when I no longer want you to

April 15th

<u>10:28PM</u>
fuck you for doing things halfway

May 4th

6:23PM

I hate you for how you tied my feelings to songs that used to be amazing and how you turned innocent kisses into sins

May 31st

<u>9:56PM</u>

I guess it‘s not my problem anymore, it‘s yours.

August 26th

5:06PM

that smile I always gave you - I breath in, look into your eyes. just a little smile, filled with all the emotions. the fact you‘re not mine and you’re never gonna be. all the love I‘ve got for you, it‘s endless. you‘re the right one, but I guess you‘re not the right one for me. but I know it‘s okay. I hope you see all of that in this smile, but you never do. I kiss you goodbye and I leave. but actually you‘re the one leaving me.

5:10PM

this is it baby. this was us.

<u>5:10PM</u>
it‘s not us anymore - it‘s you and me.

5:13PM

you‘re always going to be the one for everything.

September 1st
drunk as fuck.

I am in love with you!
I'm so deeply in love with you
I'm about to cry.
I can't handle this anymore.
I'm in so much fucking love with you.
have me
have all of me
please.
I
love
you.
real love.
this is real love.
you are real love.
How am I gonna live my life without you.
I love you. Damn I fucking love you.
your love overfills me. No, my love for you overfills me.
you don't love me.
you don't love me.

I love you, okay.
I love you.
I love you.
I could write it down all over again.
I love you. Love love love.
you're the one I truly love.

I love you.

you just texted me.
asked me why I went home so early.
I said because I was tired.
and because I like walking home with you.
(I can't tell you I love you.
but I fucking do.
do you love me?
because I love you.)
you ask me why I like going home with you.
I said because of obvious reasons.
(please love me)
you asked what reasons.
I said don't act like you don't know.
you thought because I wanted to make out with you.

(do you really not know how much I love you?)
I said no, not because of that, but okay.
(I gotta go to sleep
tomorrow I will be okay again
I gotta sleep)
I love you.

September 8th

<u>1:21AM</u>

I never got to say I love you.

October 15th
high alone at home

I wanted to love myself tonight
but then I started thinking
about you
and all I can do now
is love no one else
but you

my favorite thing to say is
in eight months you will be gone
and all my love
will go with you

once my poems were not about you
anymore
they were about me

now
they are still about me
about me
loving you.

October 26$^{th}$

<u>2:45PM</u>
this isn‘t what it could be

## November 6$^{th}$

even now
I don‘t know what‘s worse:

the fact that
you saw the love I had
for you and
used it against me

or the fact that
I let you

November $7^{th}$

<u>12:06AM</u>
I read my poems
and realized every single one is about you

over the past 2 years
I confessed my love for you several times
I always thought it was the end

12:07AM

I thought it was the end like a hundred times
but I never wanted it

this time I am writing
and hoping it finally will all be over.

12:15AM

I just read all my poems about you
I started writing them two and a half
years ago

how could I realize only now
that I loved you
from the very first day.

6:25PM

I always thought the end would be cutting
but it was slowly happening
already
when it all began.

6:29PM

I‘ve been saying thousands of words
waiting for the ones
to say it all at once.

November 17th

12:50AM
you changed once and you never will again

12:53AM

in love with the person I hate the most

December 13th

<u>8:48PM</u>

I used to think I lost you. but you don't lose something you never had.

you lost me. because you have had me all along.

December 19th

11:36PM
just for a second
I thought about texting you
and telling you I am sorry
but here I am
smoking
and I decided to write a note
instead of ruining it all
again.

11:39PM
and the worst
is
that I know no matter
how irrelevant you will be in the future
you will always
be.

December 20th

<u>6:42PM</u>

I hate every single poem about you
and not once they were about me
they were always about you
about you
and me

11:46PM

my ex texted me today
and I realized
everyone likes me
except for you.

December 29th

<u>1:03AM</u>
and every night you think to yourself
it's that time of the year
you are allowed to feel like this
and you saw him again
but you want someone else now
but it's not the new one messing with you
it's him
he is close to your heart.

# twenty nineteen

January 7th

6:11PM

I used to think about you
and feel everything all over again
and now I think about you
and you're nothing but
an emotionless memory

## January 11$^{th}$

12:18AM

here I am
still writing about you
and I hope you will miss me
in the future
so we can get together
eventually

*- I hope someday I won't write
about you when I am drunk*

## February 1st
drunk and in love

my hands are cracked
like they were a year ago
your father made a joke
why can't I let you go

my hands are cracked
like they will be in a year
in new york
I can finally let you go

let me go
you made me yours
a year ago

you don't even remember
but I do
it was a year ago
and my hands were cracked

my heart is cracked
broken apart
the skin on my hands is cracked
and it will be in new york
or maybe it won't
when my heart
isn't broken
anymore.

I'm waiting for the day
when I come home drunk
and you're not on my mind
anymore.

when my hands aren't cracked
when my heart isn't broken
when I'm in new york
and when
I'm not yours anymore.

but today isn't the day
and I am thinking of you
of us

how we were golden
but we were never meant to be together

we were golden.
but we were never meant to be together.

I will be and you will be
and you'll fly
like we were meant to be
but I will be there
with my hands cracked
in new york
with the memory of you
and no broken heart.
when you finally let me go.

February $7^{th}$

<u>11:01PM</u>

you took everything away from me
my friends
my open heart
my true self
and the part of you
which loved me.

<u>11:02PM</u>
I wanted to come home drunk
and not be thinking about you

now I came home sober
but still
all I can think about
is you.

February 17th

1:36PM

I want you to let me go
so
why
can‘t I let you go

April 7th

<u>1:46AM</u>

I hope that someday
I will come home drunk
and be filled with
happiness
because I have you
and everything I want
and this may be selfish
but all I want is
to come home drunk
and be filled with
happiness
because I have you
and everything I want
everything I want is
you.

April 22nd

12:55AM

you have been fooled
but you knew it was going to happen
you should have known better

he has been using you
for too long
maybe this was necessary
to make you realize

but you love him
and you knew it was going to hurt you
and he should have known

<u>7:23PM</u>
it is not how it is supposed to be but it is how it is

May 3rd

<u>1:01AM</u>
when I thought it was long overdue you thought it had already expired

May $25^{th}$

<u>12:40AM</u>
he probably texts her the same things
he texted me.

are you alive?

May 30$^{th}$

<u>6:07PM</u>
I want you to give me back
the piece of my heart I gave you
but on the other hand
I want you
to take all of it.

6:09PM

I don't miss you
I miss a part of you
that will never come back

I miss the way you made me feel
not the way you are

I miss myself
before you came along

and I miss that part of me;
you.

August 5th

<u>7:48PM</u>
the only downside to this entire thing is that all my poems somehow became lies

## August 13th

9:57PM
how is it
that I have it all
and I still
am not
happy?

August 15th

<u>12:51AM</u>
I have told you everything
and I don't feel bad.
all I have ever wanted
has happened
and from this moment on
I will life my life entirely
without a single spark
of you.

8:30AM

I wanted to listen to my favorite songs when you left. turns out all of them made me cry because every single one was about you. they were my favorites because they reminded me of you.

## August 23$^{rd}$
heartbroken

they all ask me
would you take him back
if he came around?
so I ask myself
would I?

I want to with
all of my heart
there is nothing I want more
than for him to come back.
this is what I want.

I would tell him to stay
or to go wherever I go
because I would go
wherever he goes.
this is what I would do.

I can give him the world
or at least I can give him mine.
but I can't give
what he doesn't take.
this is what I can do.

so I tell them
I can't take him back
even if I wanted to
because it would
break me.

so I tell them
I can't take him back
even if I wanted to
because he wouldn't even
come around.

## August 25th

11:04PM
it only took a moment
to kill four years
a moment
to kill me
and it only took a moment
for you to get over it

you are over it
and I am over

August 29th

1:03AM

I came home drunk tonight
and I didn‘t take off my makeup
like I used to years ago

and I wondered
why wasn‘t I enough?
why did you leave me?
why did you leave

and I realized
I have always been enough
I was too much
for you

and I decided
not to love you tonight
but to love me tonight

## August 31st

<u>12:08AM</u>

you never loved me. you loved it to be loved.

12:22AM

pressing forward instead of replay

12:31AM
and there I was again
staring at the ceiling
in the dark
listening to that song

and it became as empty
as it was two years ago
I became as empty
as I was two years ago

and I realized
it was you all along
it has always been you

two years ago
it stayed dark
and I wanted it to end

but today
I filled that emptiness with something
something new
something long overdue

instead of finding comfort in the dark
I started looking for the light

and unlike two years ago
I don‘t think this is how it‘ll always be
this is the beginning of something new

it may be like this now
but it won‘t be like this
forever.

I am not done.
we are.
I am not lonely.
you will be.
and I won‘t be like this forever.
but you will be.

I am going to shine
so bright it will blind you
and maybe then you will see
who I was

but then it will be too late
and the room won‘t be dark anymore
I won‘t be listening to that song
and I will be writing poems about someone else.

and they will be so much better
than those about you
because I will be better
he will be better
and everything

will shine brighter.

## September 2nd

<u>10:29PM</u>

I only miss you when I‘m drunk
do you ever miss me when you‘re drunk?

everything reminds me of you
does something ever remind you of me?

sometimes I think about texting you
do you ever want to text me?

when I‘m sad I want to call you
have you ever thought of calling me?

I do things to make you jealous
did you ever want to make me jealous?

I still care about you.
have you ever cared at all?

I miss you.
will you ever miss me?

September 11th

<u>11:05PM</u>
once I dreamt you left
I woke up and panicked
only to find out you were lying
right next to me.

I couldn't tell you
why I nearly cried that morning

last night I dreamt you stayed
I woke up and panicked
I realized you were gone
you left me.

I wish I could tell you
how much I cried this morning.

## September 13th

12:19AM

so now I‘m sitting in that bar I don‘t like
thinking about how I still love you
and you looked so pretty tonight

you hugged me tight
and asked me if we could be alright again
and I said yes

I said yes
and meant it all
I don‘t want to be alright
I want to be perfect

I want to be together
and not be waiting for food alone
I want to be with you
we are meant to be
aren’t we?

what are we going to be
is it going to be we?
am I going to leave and not come back?

am I going to find someone else?
someone better
someone like you
or someone the opposite of you

and here I am sitting in that bar I don‘t like
you looked pretty tonight
but so did I.

September $14^{th}$

on july $7^{th}$ I made a note saying “and I have never been happier”, waiting for the day I can use that sentence as an instagram caption.

since then I have written hundreds of notes, poems and stories.
never was I brave enough to use one of them as an instagram caption, neither have I ever showed them to anyone.

I don’t know if I ever will. but what I know is that out of all the things I wrote – out of all my thoughts, tears, moments in which I thought the world was going to end – the only poem I remembered almost daily was the one I kept waiting for to become true.

I kept waiting and sometimes I thought it would never come around. now I realized, by thinking of it every day for the past two years, maybe it’s not a moment. it’s a process.
maybe I can now say I have never been happier.

8:47PM
maybe I needed you.
maybe you were necessary for me to understand
how to love
how to hurt
how to forgive.

maybe I needed you.
maybe I found myself because of you
your love
your cruelty
your forgiveness.

maybe you needed me.
maybe I was the reason you discovered
you could love
you could cry
you could care.

maybe we needed each other.
maybe it was always meant to be like this.
like a movie
like a rollercoaster
like us.

maybe we were meant to be maybe.

9:02PM

thank you.
mum, for understanding what's going on before I do.
dad, for inspiring and encouraging me every day.
sister, for making me feel important.
brother, for making me smile every day.
best friend, for supporting me always.
first love, for making me see my worth.
friends, for never leaving me.
past self, for making it through.

9:20PM

first love,
thank you for helping me become who I am. I wish I could say you made me like this because it's romantic. but it was me. I made myself. because of you I had to.

thank you for being there. my past few years would have been boring without you. you made life worth living for.

thank you for seeing the spark in me almost nobody else sees, not even me. that spark set fire and we wouldn't be here if it wasn't for you.

thank you for bringing me down to earth so I could realize that you may be the first but not the only one.

*-I wouldn't have wanted it any other way*

September 15th

8:41PM
I am fine.

I am calm.
I don't know if I've ever felt like this before.

I am free and I am okay
and somehow I feel safe.
No, I am more than okay.

I am fine.

Here I am.
The woman I have always wanted to be.

I always thought this moment would come.
But I didn't know it would come this suddenly
and without any actual reason.

I am fine.

I am me.
Not depending on anyone, only enjoying.

The best thing about this is
that I am not even afraid that
everything will crash.

I am fine.

I actually feel like it's going to stay this way.

10:57PM

I tried to make the best out of you
but then it hit me like weed and gin tonic

I couldn‘t change anything about you
I also couldn‘t change the way I feel about you

So now I am making the best out of me
and it is hitting me like wine and cigarettes

## October 11th

<u>11:18PM</u>
I'm in bed and I imagined
your arms wrapping around me
but I felt the need to push them away

and then I thought I'm glad
I'm alone in my bed
so you cannot
push me away.

October 15th

<u>11:41PM</u>

do you sometimes think of me
because I think of you
sometimes.

what made you go away from me
if you said
it wasn't me?

why do I imagine myself with someone
I don't even know yet
but somehow he looks like you?

how do I tell everyone I'm fine
why do I actually believe I'm fine
when I could cry when I think of you
with someone else
that doesn't look like me?

October 16th

12:00AM

sometimes I wonder, if I had begged you on my knees for you to stay. if I had tried to convince you we are working out. if I had reminded you of all the good things. if I hadn‘t cried. if I would have kissed you a little longer. if I had worn the sweater you like. if I hadn‘t made you come to my house that night.

would you have stayed?

sometimes I wonder, because I haven‘t begged you on my knees for you to stay. because I haven‘t tried to convince you we are working out. because I didn‘t remind you of all the good things. because I cried. because I didn‘t even want to kiss you. because I threw away the sweater you like. because I made you come to my house that night.

did I even want you to stay?

maybe I didn't just accept you leaving. maybe I made you, because I unconsciously wanted you to. I was kinda unhappy anyway because I was in constant fear of losing you again. you may have left me, but maybe, just maybe, for once, I had already left you first.

October 19th

<u>8:33PM</u>
I‘m thinking
I would give a lot to talk to you one more time
but what
would I even say to you?

I still feel the same way
I did two months ago
when I already told you
everything.

November 3rd

<u>3:49AM</u>
okay so
this was a terrible misunderstanding
and I could literally cry right know
because I never meant to hurt anyone
not her
not you
I don't know what it sounded like to you
but how wrong can you be
if you think someone like me
wouldn't care
but I feel like
you want this to pin on me
so you have a reason
to be mad
and a reason
to have broken up with me

December 5th

<u>3:01PM</u>

at the end of the year, for some reason, I ended up where I wanted to be at the beginning of it.

December 16th

2:13PM
it feels wrong to write
and writing about you
has never felt wrong

I am over you
and I realized I don't write anymore
you were all I wrote about

I think I have always been a writer
but you awakened the poet in me

and when you left my mind
you took my poems with you.

December 26th

10:48PM
when will I not want you
when will I want someone else
and not you.

what did you do to me?
you're not good.
not at all.

but damn.
I miss you.
and I want you.
you were the first.
and I think you will always be
not only the first
but the one.

but you never wanted me.
not once.
not ever.

twenty
twenty

## January 1st

8:13PM

I thought I needed you to be complete
I thought I needed you to have it all
but I don't.

I thought I wanted you to love me
I thought I couldn't love myself
but I can.

I have it all
even though I don't have you.

but you don't have me anymore either
I still have myself though
and so much more

only now I know I didn't need you
to have it all.

January 4th

I keep wondering what I'll feel when I'll listen to the songs I'm listening to now in a few months. because now I'm kind of in between emotions.

I still think of him sometimes but I feel nothing when I do. I'm not hurt anymore, I don't love him anymore, I don't need him anymore. his name is just worth three letters of nothing. I don't even hate him. it's just empty.

when I think of the next few months I get excited at first, quickly followed by a deep fear of not being able to go. I'm afraid I'll die first, get involved in an accident or just anything which will make me unable to go. there is nothing I care about more than this.

I'm just hoping everything will turn out for the best. this year I want to be successful and work for it. I would like to find some kind of love but I'm not going to force anything. I believe I'm lovable.

January $7^{th}$

<u>10:22PM</u>
for quite some time
when I knew I was over him
I questioned my love for him
like
did I ever really love him?
did I truly love him
if I could get over him like this?

but then that song came on shuffle
and I realized
I did.

- *but I don't anymore*

10:48PM

I don't know why I'm thinking of you today. like, it's not that I miss you or feel like texting you and need something to distract me. and it's different this time anyway. I'm on the couch instead of my bed, I write in english instead of swiss german, I am not writing on paper so I could give it to you one day. I'm in a whole different house, which I really don't like by the way. I'm not home here.

anyway, I hope you're doing well. I really do. but you already know I never wanted you to feel unwell and I never will. I hope you think of me sometimes though or speak highly of me when people ask you about me, even though you probably don't. I'd like to know if you kissed other girls after me because I surely kissed other boys.

thank god I did, because one of them actually really helped me get over you. never thought that would happen, but oh well, years ago I thought I could never fall in love with you and look where this ended up.

oh and please don't rub my back when you hug me. I'm totally fine and don't need comfort from the person who broke me in the first place.

## January 24th

12:12AM
the thing is
every time I feel lonely
or when I want to feel loved
I think of you.

It took me a while to realize
It's not because I miss you
or because I still love you
it's because I used to

you're the only person
I ever truly loved with
all of my heart

I don't think love is a feeling
I think love is the person who means everything
and you meant everything to me.

12:49AM

I don't know you anymore
when I try to picture your face
I only see a silhouette

when I try to hear your voice
the music is louder

when we hug I feel uncomfortable
and don't feel the need to pull you closer
I don't know you anymore.

I know the person you used to be.

January 25th

9:21PM
Fuck it.
I don't think I ever got over you.
I just moved on.

January 31st

12:17AM
I'm leaving for new york tomorrow
I texted them both
because I really miss them both

this is what I've been waiting for
and I feel like it's been waiting for me.

I'm leaving tomorrow
and I don't even know what I'm feeling right now

I'm enough
and more than that
I made it
I'm going to new york.
I am okay.

## February 14th

10:37PM

I used to think someday I will only have memories of you and have no emotions attached to them. but now I'm trying to remember our moments and there's nothing. I don't know who you are. I don't know what you do in your spare time, where your favorite place is or if you sleep with the windows opened or closed. I don't know what you want to do with your life, do you want kids someday?

you said you would never have kids with me if I got to choose the names. you sent me a christmas card with erased pencil lines saying you never want to lose me and that you love me with all of your heart. I know you sleep with your socks on, I know you don't wet your toothbrush before using it. I know you liked my mum. I know you cared about me passing the year. I know you missed me.

when I asked you if you ever said I love you and meant it, you said no.

I hoped it was a lie or that you just forgot. but no one forgets when they loved someone.

the most love I ever felt from you was when you broke up with me.

February 29th

12:38PM
tomorrow is a new day.
tomorrow you can invent a new you.
tomorrow is not today and
tomorrow will bring something you don't know about yet.
tomorrow is just as close as it's far,
tomorrow can be just as good or bad as today was
because let's be honest,
tomorrow is sunday and hangovers are real.
tomorrow might be plannable but not everything is going to be as you planned it to be.
tomorrow is a mystery.
tomorrow you're a day closer to what you've been waiting for and
tomorrow you're a day further away of what you've been trying to forget.
tomorrow, not going to lie, is probably going to be just another day.
tomorrow is going to happen, whether all this wannabe deep stuff matters or not
tomorrow is what you make it.

March 6$^{th}$

3:04AM

I am in a good place.

March 18th

11:17PM
for the past week
the sentence bouncing in my head
has been

I am not supposed to be here

over there everything made sense
getting up in the morning
I was doing this for me

here I am going back into bad habits
drinking myself to sleep
smoking until my lungs turn black
texting him

I am not supposed to be here

I am supposed to be someone else

## March 22nd

6:46PM

I can‘t make you fall in love with me

you might be the one for me
but I am not the one for you.

the same way I don‘t know why it feels like you belong to me even though you‘re nothing like everything I imagine

you can‘t find reasons to actually love me and want me forever

some things are just the way they are
and we might have been meant to be

but we were never meant to be together.

7:14PM

I don't want to be here
I am not supposed to be here

I am not supposed to be the person I am here
I want to be someone else
without you

I am so much better off without you
but how the fuck do I tell my heart that

and how do I tell you that
when I really want you to want me

April 5th

10:26PM
I say I am confused
and I am

I am confused about everything
I don't understand any of this
and maybe I never will

and that's okay

because I know this is wrong
but I also know that I want you

no matter how this ends
if it even does end one day

you are going to break my heart again
and I am just going to let you.

April 15th

12:55AM
and there it is
the moment I realize

fuck.

I fell in love all over again

May 14th

10:55PM
you said marrying me wasn't on the table
yet

and I'm wondering if those three letters
are worth trying again.

May 26th

8:01PM
I‘m 19
why am I so afraid of never finding love?

I keep telling myself I‘m lovable, but for some reason no one has ever seen the world in my eyes. no one will buy me flowers, will want to spend time with me, not even be bothered if I don‘t text back for some reason. when I say it‘s okay even though it really is not and I just don‘t have the energy to explain because it will lead to nothing anyway, no one asks if it really is okay.

I downplay my feelings, keep quiet when something is bothering me, I say „it doesn‘t matter, all good“ way too often. just because I‘m afraid getting into a fight will make me lose them.

I understand if you don‘t love somebody, that‘s just the way it is. a person can be just too perfect and still there might not be that feeling. I understand.

I keep dreaming of getting married unhappily, getting cheated on or my soulmate forgetting my birthday. the words „I never said I love you and meant it“ keep spinning in my head.

I‘m so afraid of being vulnerable, opening up to someone, initiating the relationship talk. I don‘t ever wanna get hurt again.

I daydream about someone randomly calling me, showing up at my house, texting me if I wanna go for a drive, someone telling me I‘m beautiful when I didn‘t even try. someone telling their friends how proud they are to have me. someone whose eyes light up when they say my name.

I‘m 19
and I‘m afraid being so scared of never finding love will make me stop from finding love.

June 1st

<u>10:35PM</u>
back to when drinking was a desire
not a need

when smoking was a relief
not an addiction

when randomly knocking on your friend's door was only a minute away
(or two, considering how long the elevators took)

when dream was reality

when I was the person I always wanted to be

where I was where I always wanted to be

when everything was how it was supposed to be.

June 21st

20:49PM

I had a hundred speeches ready in my head in case you ever came up to me and actually wanted to talk to me about what was going on. of course, you didn't, that's how you always do it. you always slowly disappear out of my life instead of communicating like a normal grownup. you think you don't owe people an explanation or closure and usually I would say that's true but in this case it's just fucked up. at this point I know you and to be honest I'm almost grateful we never had that talk because I don't know what I would've said. half of my speeches end with „but I still wanna do this“ and the other half with „and that's why I never ever want to do this again.“ even though I don't mind we never talked I'm still pissed off because you treated me like this again. I refused to start the talk myself because I am not running after you anymore. I don't know what I expected you to do but just let me say I wasn't surprised by the way you acted like when we were 16 again. anyway -

I want you to like me. actually like me. you should want to spend time with me, you should want to be on your phone more often when that's the only way we can communicate. you should actually care when I tell you something's bothering me and you should ask me if I want to do something together the next day. when getting into a relationship it's not „I wanna try." you shouldn't even want to think about the option of this not working out, I am not an experiment. I am not a label, I'm not only your girlfriend and that's it. I should be a priority. a relationship means effort. and I am not giving everything and not getting anything back anymore. I can't carry this alone. if you actually wanted me you wouldn't mind putting in that effort. actually... if you really wanted me I wouldn't have to tell you all of this in the first place. I don't need to teach you how to be in a relationship. it should come naturally. I can't enter a relationship when I am doubting it before it even starts. I don't want you anymore. I want the idea of you, the idea of a relationship and being loved.

but you could never give me that love. and that's why I never ever wanna do this again.

the question has never been asked but my answer is still no. I just don't know if I'll be able to say that word if you ever decide to tell me you want me. so I hope you never do.

July 8th

<u>12:01AM</u>

I've wanted sex the past few weeks
more than I usually do

and I was actually proud of myself
for just wanting sex and nothing more

but do I really only want physical love
when I always get
emotionally attached
to everyone giving me
the slightest amount of love?

July $10^{th}$

12:25AM

I'd rather hurt myself
by letting them go before it even gets good

instead of letting them hurt me
after it got good.

July 29th

12:21AM

I was afraid there was never gonna be someone

who is gonna want me the way I wanted you

but there are gonna be plenty of those people

what if I am never gonna want someone again the way I wanted you?

August 12th

<u>10:09PM</u>
how did you manage to talk about your feelings when you never even had any

10:30PM

I was out
and you texted me if I wanted to fuck the next day
my friend saw your message, ripped the phone out of my hands and sent „no“
I was confused for a second because I wouldn‘t have said it that way

I don‘t even know what I would‘ve said
but I‘m glad she started my messages with that word
because I should‘ve said it so much time ago

when I asked you to come over you never showed up
when I wanted to fuck you didn‘t bother to get in the car,
I wasn‘t even good enough for that

but when you‘re horny you expect me to show up at your door

I told you this.

I want a relationship, more than sex, someone who cares when I cry.
you misunderstood and thought I wanted a relationship with you and asked me what all that „this is just sex“ was about. I don‘t want a relationship with you. I don‘t want sex with you. I don‘t want you at all. I‘m done.

I told you this.

you said thank you for everything
and I said what?
this was so much more for me than it ever was for you
and you said well, for being a really good friend and experiencing lots of firsts with me.
I said well there you go, you were way more than a really good friend to me.

I told you this.

you asked if we could still keep the contact
and I said that's what you said too when you broke up
with me last year
you said that was different
I said we were never any different than today and what
we've been for the past four years
you said that's true

you said you have the feeling that this is over now.
I immediately sent „yes“ without doubting or being afraid
I'd regret it.

we said good night
I put away my phone
I curled up under the sheets
and started crying
I could feel weight falling off my shoulders
I said no.
finally.

thank you.